Complete Edition | Later Elementary to Early Intermediate

NEW ORLEANS
JAZZ STYLES
SIMPLIFIED

By William Gillock
Adapted by Glenda Austin

T0079337

ISBN 978-1-70511-393-6

EXCLUSIVELY DISTRIBUTED BY

© 2020 by The Willis Music Co.
International Copyright Secured   All Rights Reserved

For all works contained herein:
Unauthorized copying, arranging, adapting, recording, internet posting, public performance,
or other distribution of the music in this publication is an infringement of copyright.
Infringers are liable under the law.

Visit Hal Leonard Online at
www.halleonard.com

Contact us:
Hal Leonard
7777 West Bluemound Road
Milwaukee, WI 53213
Email: info@halleonard.com

In Europe, contact:
Hal Leonard Europe Limited
42 Wigmore Street
Marylebone, London, W1U 2RN
Email: info@halleonardeurope.com

In Australia, contact:
Hal Leonard Australia Pty. Ltd.
4 Lentara Court
Cheltenham, Victoria, 3192 Australia
Email: info@halleonard.com.au

PREFACE

The *Simplified New Orleans Jazz* pieces were first published in 2001. I wanted to include the original preface below. I am re-reading it in 2020, and there is not really a lot to add: it already covers it all. You will notice tweaks in this edition that were made to simplify certain pieces just a little more. (You may or may not even notice them!) According to Webster, *simplify* means: "to make simple or simpler: such as to reduce to basic essentials." By simplifying, perhaps more students will discover jazz at an earlier stage in their study.

Glenda Austin

November 2020

I first met William Gillock in the summer of 1980. Over the years we visited many times in each other's home, at conventions and workshops, and by telephone. I treasure those occasions because, to me, Bill became not only a mentor and teacher, but also a genuinely kind-hearted and true friend who continues to inspire me to this day.

Bill spoke often of his earlier years, his love and appreciation of music and the fine arts, his life in New Orleans, and his fondness for jazz. I recall hearing him conclude workshops with his rendition of "Frankie and Johnny" and the audience absolutely loving it!

In his *New Orleans Jazz Styles* collections, Bill provided teachers and students with original jazz pieces of intermediate level. It has been a pleasure and joy to arrange them in simplified form. Now, more students may experience their introduction to jazz at an earlier age.

May this be the beginning of a lifelong enjoyment to a great American development – jazz!

Thank you, Bill.

CONTENTS

New Orleans Nightfall

William Gillock
Adapted by Glenda Austin

Song style; somewhat flexibly, with a swing feel

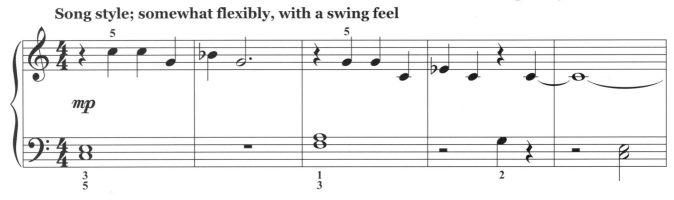

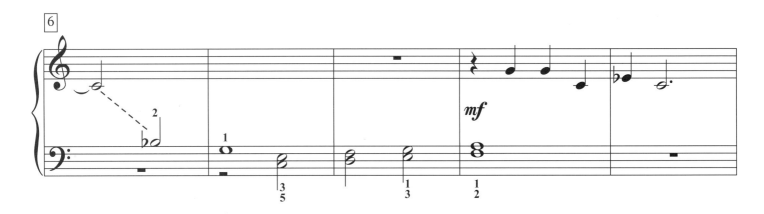

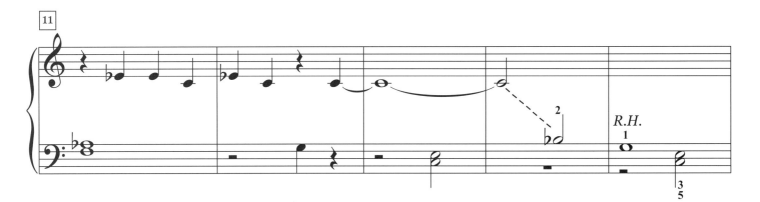

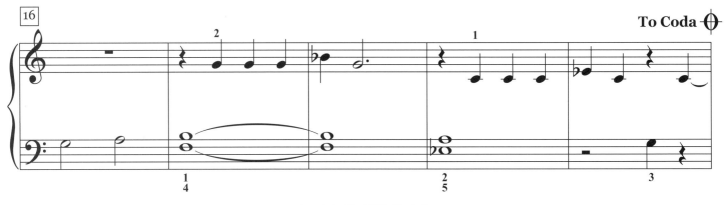

© 1965 by The Willis Music Co.
Copyright Renewed
This arrangement © 2001 by The Willis Music Co.
International Copyright Secured All Rights Reserved

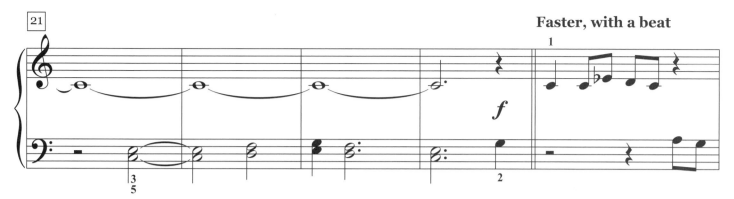

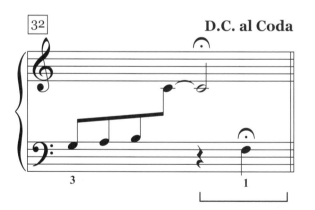

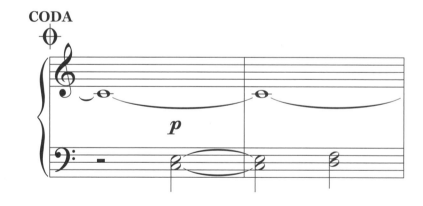

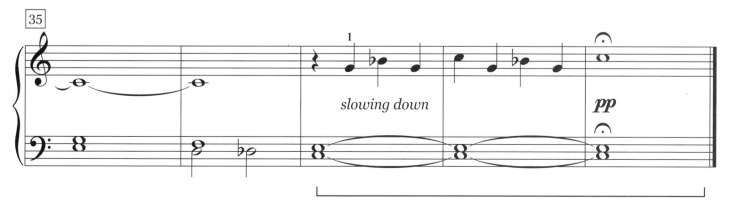

The Constant Bass

William Gillock
Adapted by Glenda Austin

Steady beat

Play R.H. 8va on repeat

L.H. staccato throughout

To Coda

© 1965 by The Willis Music Co.
Copyright Renewed
This arrangement © 2001 by The Willis Music Co.
International Copyright Secured   All Rights Reserved

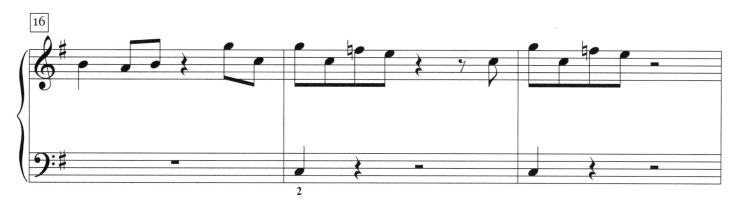

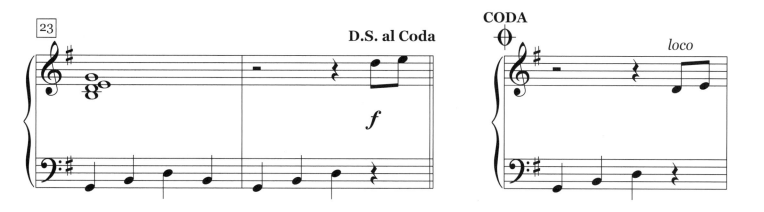

D.S. al Coda

CODA

Dixieland Combo

William Gillock
Adapted by Glenda Austin

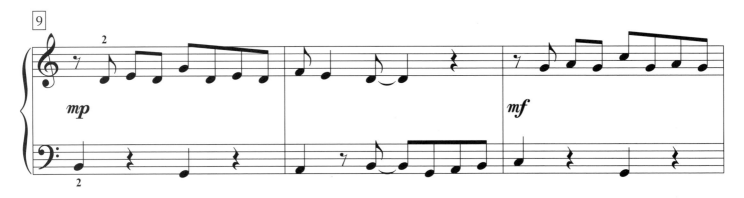

© 1965 by The Willis Music Co.
Copyright Renewed
This arrangement © 2001 by The Willis Music Co.
International Copyright Secured   All Rights Reserved

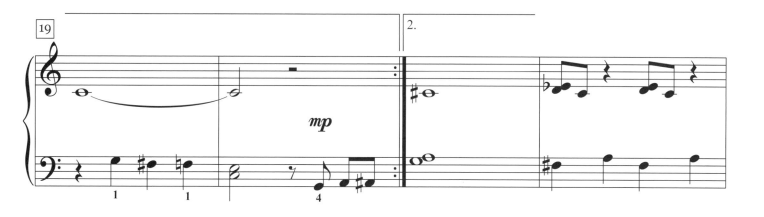

Frankie and Johnny
Theme and Variations

William Gillock
Adapted by Glenda Austin

Bold and bluesy

© 1965 by The Willis Music Co.
Copyright Renewed
This arrangement © 2001 by The Willis Music Co.
International Copyright Secured All Rights Reserved

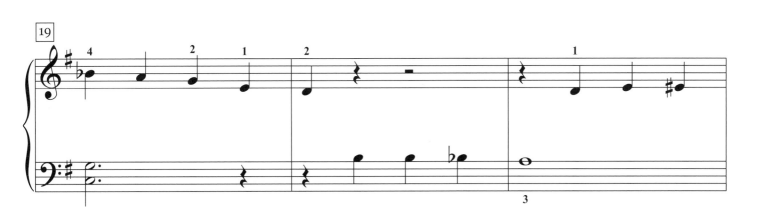

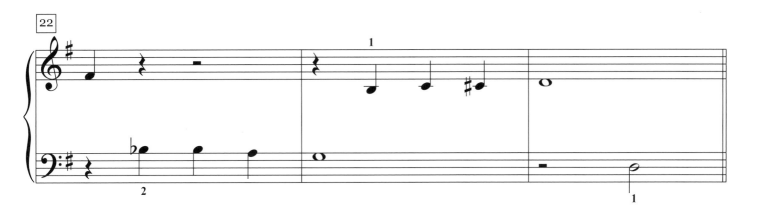

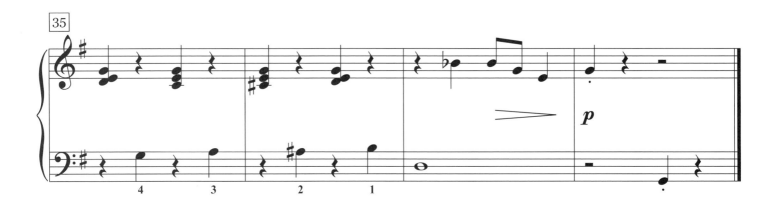

Mardi Gras

William Gillock
Adapted by Glenda Austin

Hurried

Play R.H. 8va on repeat

© 1965 by The Willis Music Co.
Copyright Renewed
This arrangement © 2001 by The Willis Music Co.
International Copyright Secured   All Rights Reserved

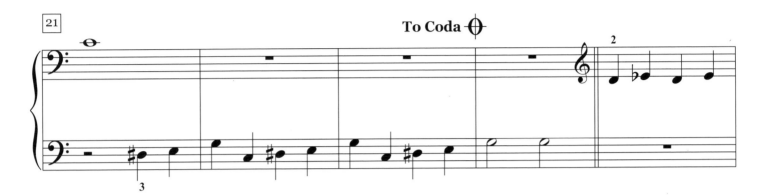

To Coda ⊕

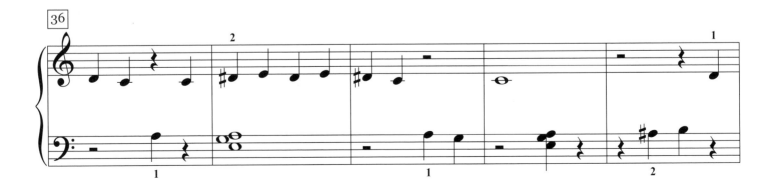

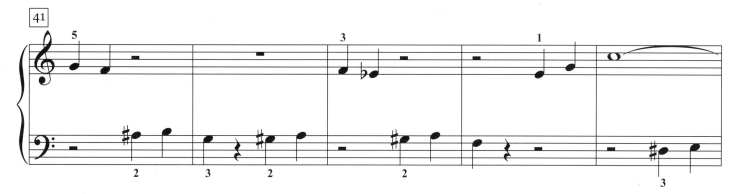

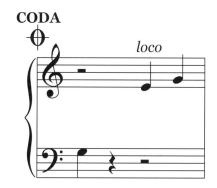

D.S. al Coda

CODA

loco

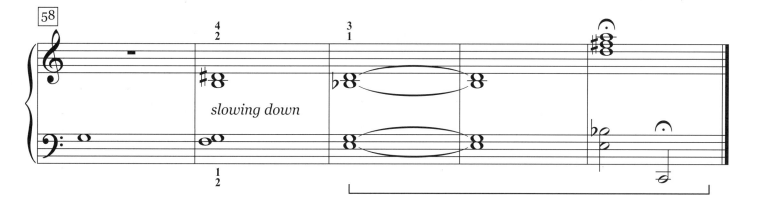

slowing down

Taking It Easy

William Gillock
Adapted by Glenda Austin

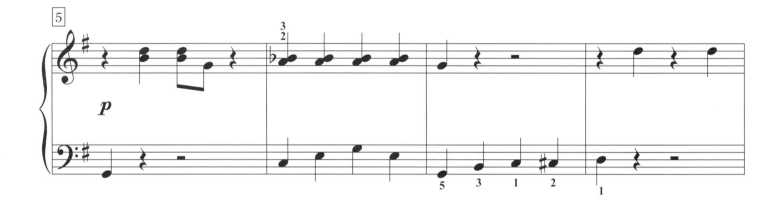

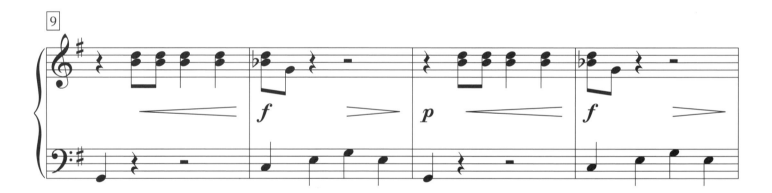

© 1965 by The Willis Music Co.
Copyright Renewed
This arrangement © 2001 by The Willis Music Co.
International Copyright Secured   All Rights Reserved

After Midnight

William Gillock
Adapted by Glenda Austin

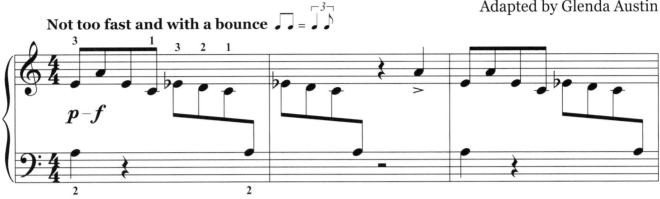

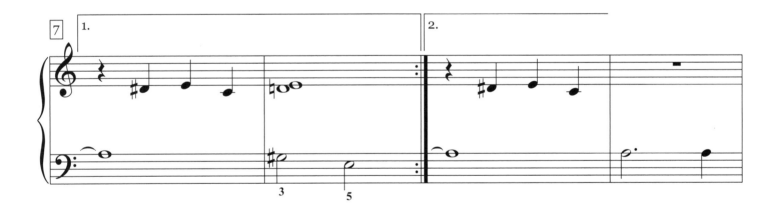

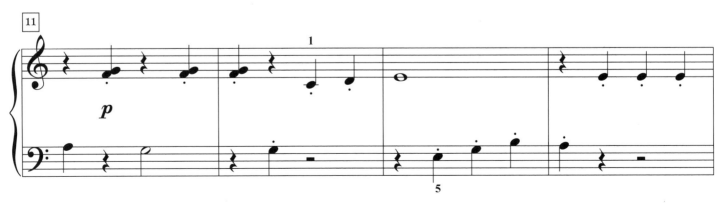

© 1965 by The Willis Music Co.
Copyright Renewed
This arrangement © 2001 by The Willis Music Co.
International Copyright Secured   All Rights Reserved

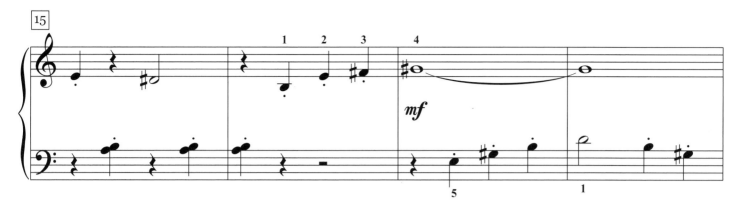

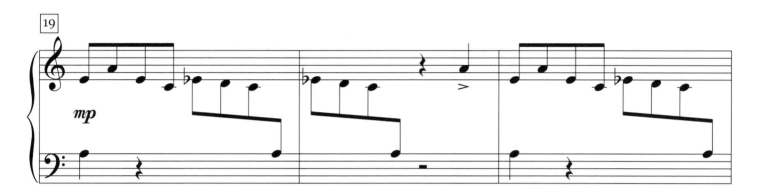

Mister Trumpet Man

William Gillock
Adapted by Glenda Austin

© 1965 by The Willis Music Co.
Copyright Renewed
This arrangement © 2001 by The Willis Music Co.
International Copyright Secured   All Rights Reserved

D.C. al Coda

Bourbon Street Saturday Night

William Gillock
Adapted by Glenda Austin

© 1965 by The Willis Music Co.
Copyright Renewed
This arrangement © 2001 by The Willis Music Co.
International Copyright Secured   All Rights Reserved

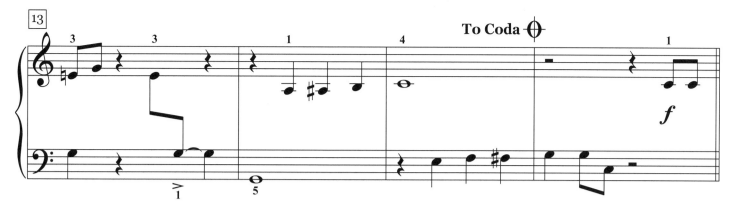

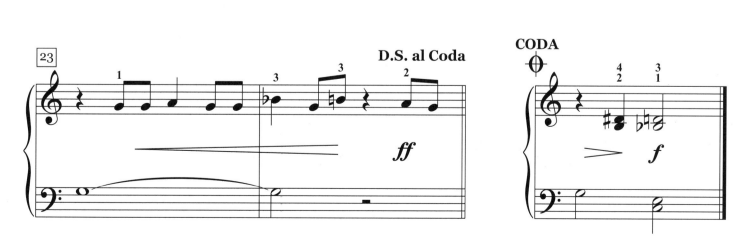

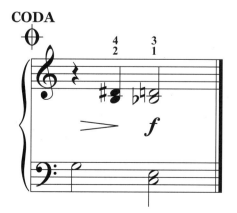

New Orleans Blues

William Gillock
Adapted by Glenda Austin

Slow Blues tempo, with a swing feel

𝄋 *Play R.H. 8va on repeat*

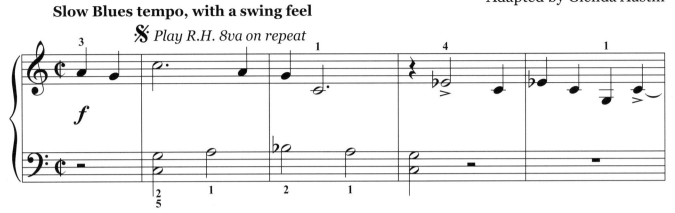

© 1965 by The Willis Music Co.
Copyright Renewed
This arrangement © 2001 by The Willis Music Co.
International Copyright Secured   All Rights Reserved

To Coda

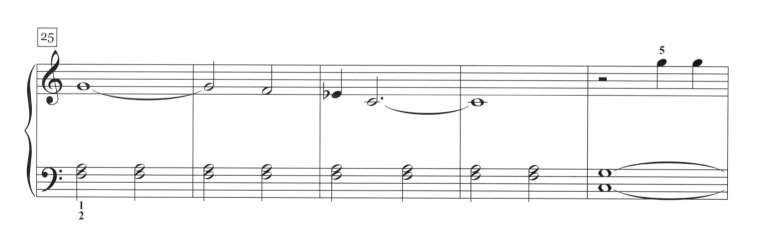

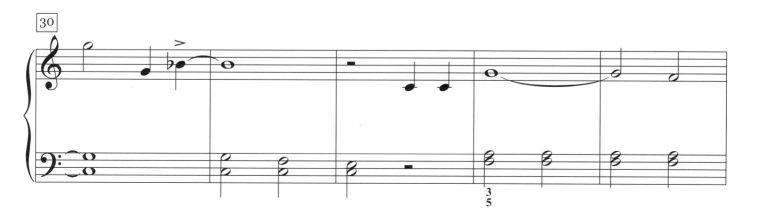

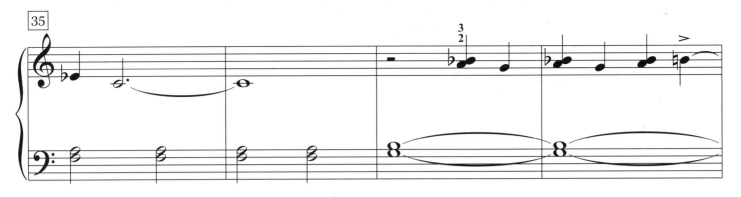

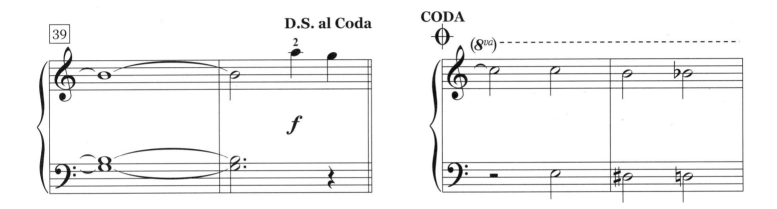

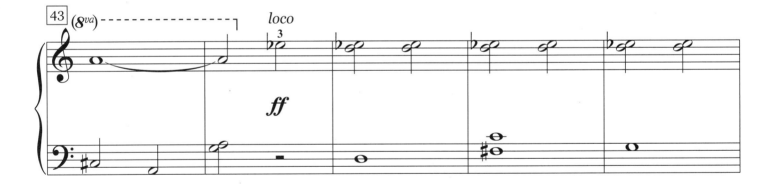

Mississippi Mud

William Gillock
Adapted by Glenda Austin

Lazily, with a swing feel

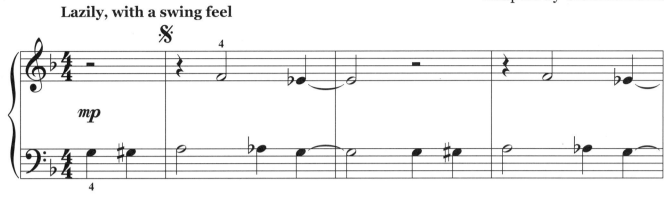

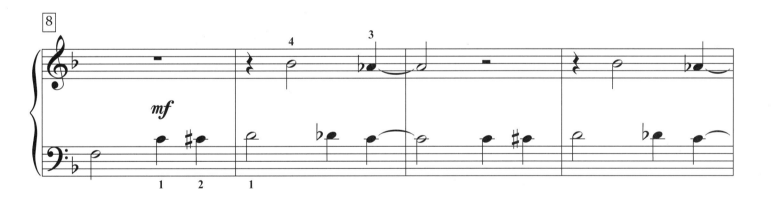

© 1965 by The Willis Music Co.
Copyright Renewed
This arrangement © 2001 by The Willis Music Co.
International Copyright Secured   All Rights Reserved

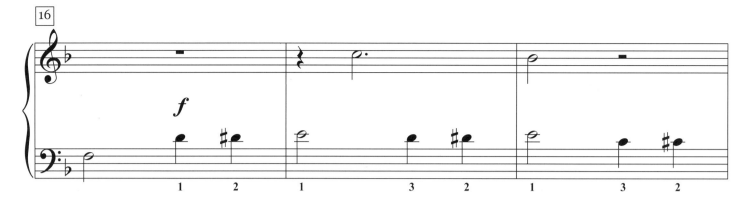

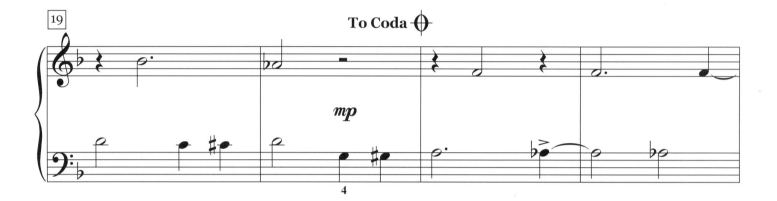

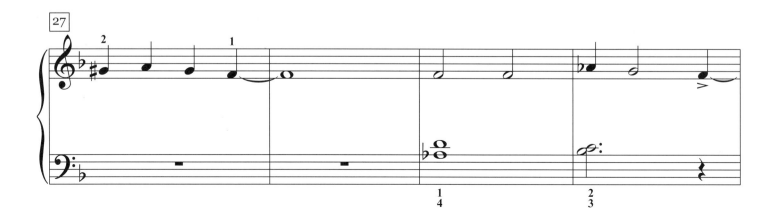

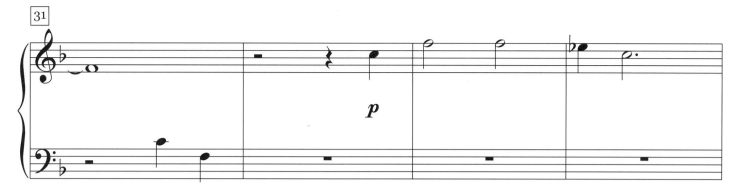

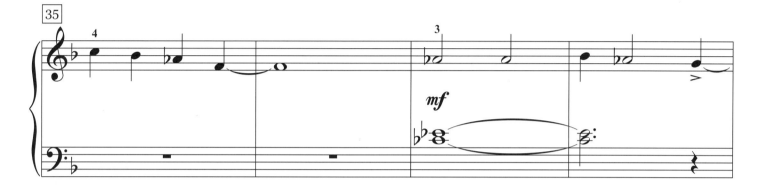

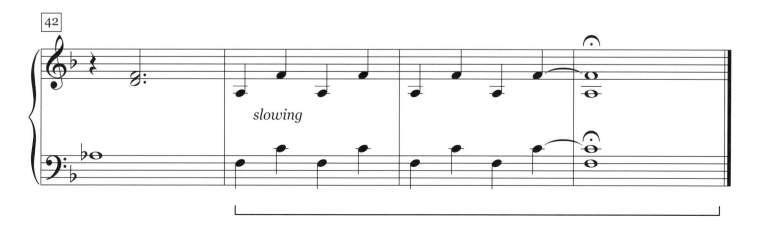

Uptown Blues

William Gillock
Adapted by Glenda Austin

Smoothly, with a swing feel

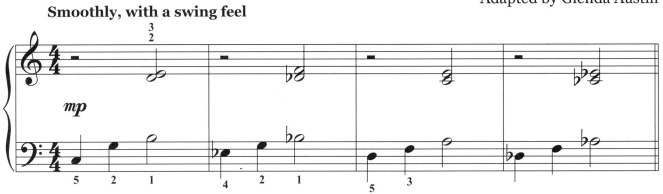

Play R.H. 8va on repeat

© 1965 by The Willis Music Co.
Copyright Renewed
This arrangement © 2001 by The Willis Music Co.
International Copyright Secured   All Rights Reserved

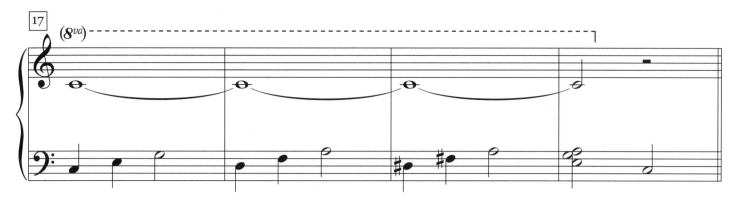

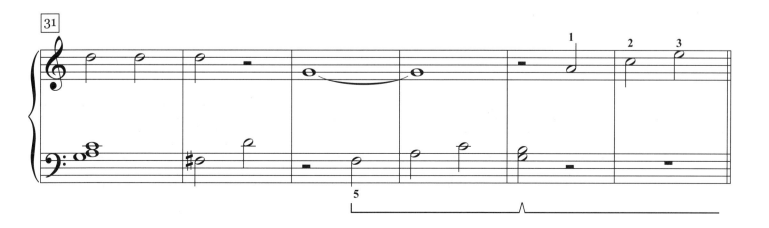

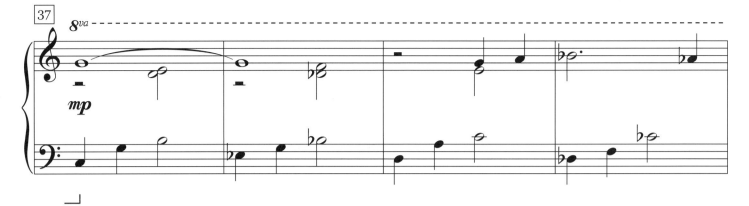

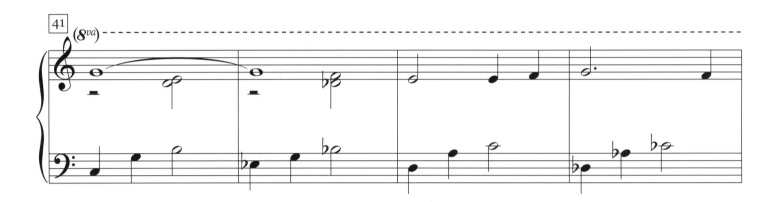

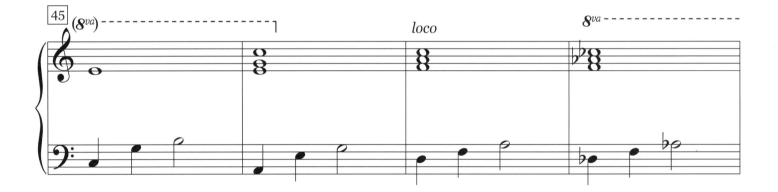

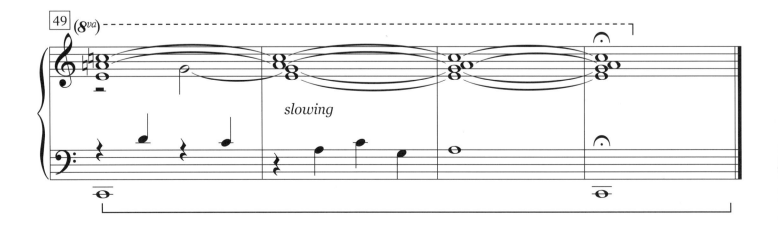

Canal Street Blues

William Gillock
Adapted by Glenda Austin

Moderately, with a swing feel

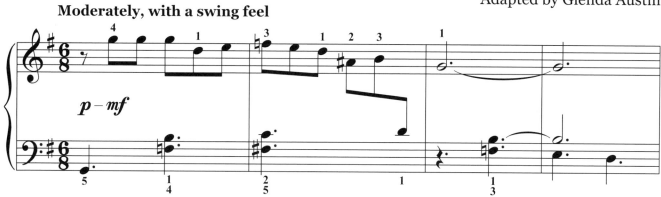

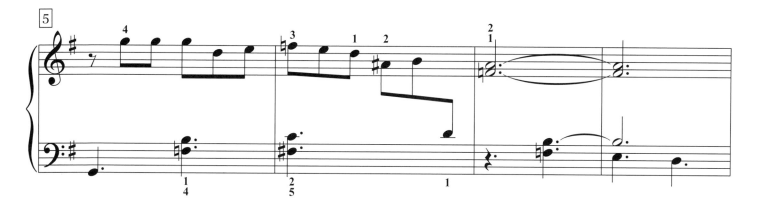

© 1965 by The Willis Music Co.
Copyright Renewed
This arrangement © 2001 by The Willis Music Co.
International Copyright Secured   All Rights Reserved

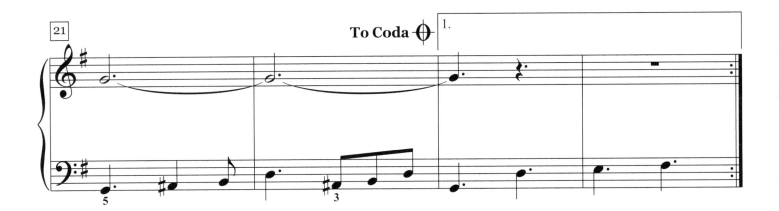

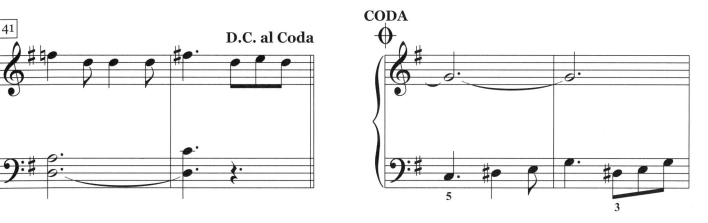

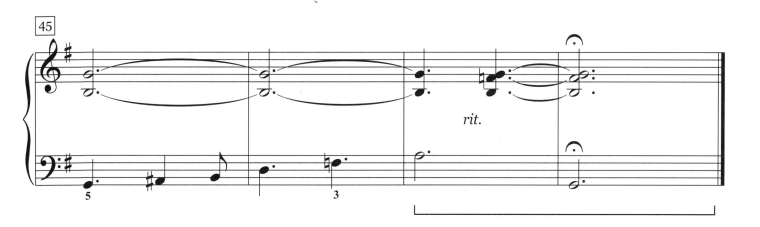

Downtown Beat

William Gillock
Adapted by Glenda Austin

Intensely rhythmic, in 2, with a swing feel

Play R.H. 8va on repeat

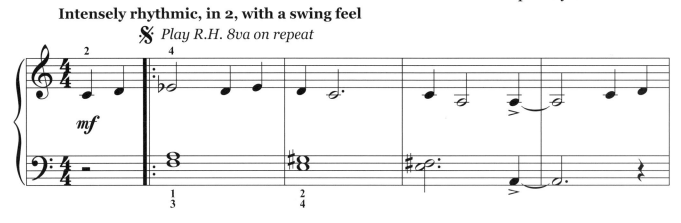

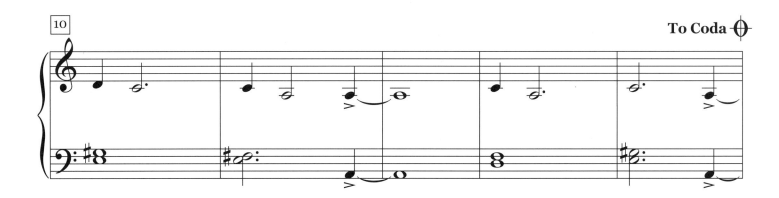

To Coda ⊕

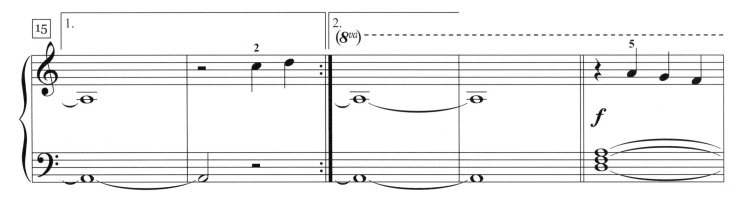

© 1965 by The Willis Music Co.
Copyright Renewed
This arrangement © 2001 by The Willis Music Co.
International Copyright Secured   All Rights Reserved

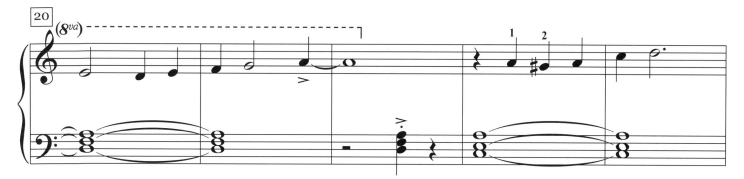

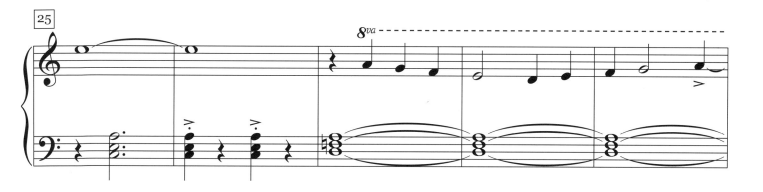

D.S. al Coda
(loco)

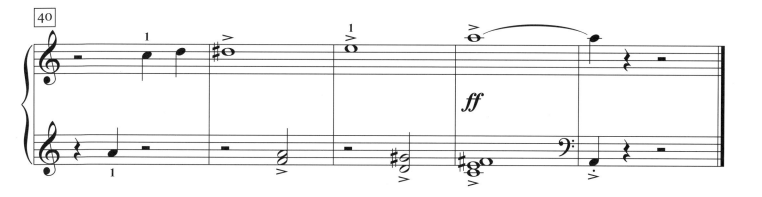

Bill Bailey

Hugh Cannon
Arranged by William Gillock
Adapted by Glenda Austin

Bright bounce tempo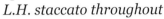

L.H. staccato throughout

Play R.H. 8va on repeat

© 1965 by The Willis Music Co.
Copyright Renewed
This arrangement © 2001 by The Willis Music Co.
International Copyright Secured   All Rights Reserved

loco both times

WILLIAM GILLOCK (1917–1993), noted music educator and composer of piano music, was born in LaRussell, Missouri, where he learned to play the piano at an early age. After graduating from Central Methodist College, his musical career led him to long tenures in New Orleans, Louisiana and Dallas, Texas, where he was always in great demand as a teacher, clinician, and composer. Called the "Schubert of children's composers" in tribute to his extraordinary melodic gift, Gillock composed numerous solos and ensembles for students of all levels. He was honored on multiple occasions by the National Federation of Music Clubs (NFMC) with the Award of Merit for Service to American Music, and his music continues to be remarkably popular throughout the United States and throughout the world.

GLENDA AUSTIN is a composer, arranger, and pianist from Joplin, Missouri. She is a graduate of the University of Missouri in Columbia, where she earned a B.S. in music education and a M.M. in piano performance. Austin recently retired from teaching general music in public and private schools but continues to perform for community theater and church. She is an adjunct faculty member of Missouri Southern State University and serves as pianist for various chamber and concert choirs. In addition, she is an active clinician for Willis Music and has presented clinics and showcases nationally, as well as in Canada and Japan. Her works are consistently placed on the National Federation of Music Clubs Junior Festival list, and she has been commissioned as a composer by *Clavier* magazine, as well as several independent teacher organizations.

Bill and Glenda circa 1980.